THE HOLE

A Play in One Act

by

N. F. SIMPSON

LONDON

SAMUEL FRENCH LIMITED

SAMUEL FRENCH LTD
26 SOUTHAMPTON STREET, STRAND, LONDON

SAMUEL FRENCH INC
25 WEST 45TH STREET, NEW YORK
7623 SUNSET BOULEVARD, HOLLYWOOD

SAMUEL FRENCH (CANADA) LTD
27 GRENVILLE STREET, TORONTO

SAMUEL FRENCH (AUSTRALIA) PTY LTD
ELIZABETHAN THEATRE TRUST BUILDING
133 DOWLING STREET, SYDNEY

822.91

Printed in Great Britain by
Latimer Trend & Co Ltd Whitstable

THE HOLE

Produced at the Royal Court Theatre, London, on the 2nd April, 1958, with the following cast of characters:

(in the order of their appearance)

THE VISIONARY	*Toke Townley*
ENDO	*Robert Stephens*
CEREBRO	*Philip Locke*
SOMA	*Nigel Davenport*
MRS MESO	*Sheila Ballantine*
MRS ECTO	*Avril Elgar*
WORKMAN	*Jon Rollason*

Directed by WILLIAM GASKILL
Décor by STANLEY RIXON

The action of the Play passes around a hole dug in the road

THE HOLE

SCENE—*A hole dug in the road.*

> *The hole is C of a run of low rostra down stage. There is a pavement at the same level immediately above the hole, from which steps at the left end lead up to a pavement at a higher level, where there is a short length of railings overlooking the lower pavement and the hole. A ramp back C leads down and off from the higher pavement. The hole is marked off by barriers; a pole supported by wooden tripods at the back, and tubular rails on the other three sides. Immediately down L of the hole is an empty upturned oil bin, used as a seat. Inside the barrier there are two oil lamps and a red flag is on the left end of the barrier pole.*
>
> *(See the Ground Plan at the end of the Play)*

When the CURTAIN rises, a man is lying R of the hole, wrapped in a blanket. He has with him a camp stool; an air cushion; a haversack containing some books, writing paper and pencil; an alarm clock; a newspaper and a vacuum flask full of tea. There is an air of patient single-mindedness about him, but although he peers from time to time through the barrier with fascinated interest, it is only at the preparations going on, unseen by anyone else, for the event to which he has dedicated every otherwise ineffectual part of himself. He deserves, for his pertinacity, to be referred to as the VISIONARY. The alarm goes off. The VISIONARY fumblingly switches it off, rises, folds the blanket, opens the camp stool, sits on it and pours himself some tea from the vacuum flask. ENDO crosses briskly from L to R past the Visionary, sees him, checks, returns, watches him for a moment, and then begins asking him questions.

ENDO.   Are you expecting anything special to happen?

VISIONARY.   I'm forming the nucleus of a queue.

ENDO. Just waiting. In the abstract, as you might say. (*He stands looking at the Visionary for a few moments*) There seems to be no-one else in the queue.

VISIONARY. Perhaps they have queues of their own.

ENDO. Don't you think it's likely someone will join you later?

VISIONARY. There will in all probability be no others. It isn't of any importance.

ENDO. Just the nucleus?

VISIONARY. It's enough. My ambition once was to have a queue stretching away from me in every possible direction known to the compass. I meant in those days, God willing, to have queues radiating out from me like the spikes from a prison railing. Like nodules endlessly attenuated. If I'd had my way then you could probably have detonated me like a mine simply by touching one of them, dangerous though it would have been. At least one queue would have been forming vertically and I saw myself being slowly crushed to death under the weight of it. What a consummation of my hopes and ambitions that would have been. To be first in an infinity of queues! Cosmically first! Omniprimal!

ENDO. But you gave up the idea.

VISIONARY. The nucleus is enough for me now. No more than that is needed. I am satisfied to queue in solitude.

ENDO. How long eventually do you think you will have to have waited?

VISIONARY. For what?

ENDO. For—well, what is it you're queueing for?

VISIONARY. This is a small queue which has been forming for weeks, months, years, decades, centuries, millenia, aeons, days and indeed for some hours now and is made up of people who are determined to be here the moment the proceedings start and to be moreover the first to be on the scene when things begin to happen so that they miss nothing by arriving after the ceremony has got under way through not having formed the nucleus of a queue the day before yesterday or two minutes ago or last year or when Charlemagne was alive or at some

Photograph by Roger Mayne

To face page 2— The Hole

other convenient moment before the solemn unveiling of the great window in the south transept whose quote or rather misquote many-coloured glass will God willing in all probability stain the white radiance of eternity unquote to the everlasting glory of God.

ENDO. And how do you keep warm these cold nights?

VISIONARY. I have an electric blanket. (*He peers into the hole*)

ENDO. Isn't that rather heavy on electricity? Where do you plug it in?

VISIONARY. I generate my own.

ENDO. That must keep you rather busy.

VISIONARY. Only while I'm doing it.

ENDO. Perhaps it helps to pass the time. I should think the days must go by very slowly for you.

VISIONARY. I've never timed them. (*He leans forward and peers into the hole*)

ENDO. And food. How do you manage about food? Do you get enough to eat and drink while you sit here?

(*The* VISIONARY *sits up*)

Isn't it a bit of a problem, the catering?

VISIONARY. I thought I saw a movement among the congregation. They're all in their places down there. It's just a matter of waiting now. They're sitting most of them in the south transept itself, where they can see the full effect of the sun striking the glass when they unveil the window. It won't be long—you'll see something happening in a moment if you watch.

(*There is a pause.* ENDO *looks down into the hole. His attention is momentarily engaged by something going on down there*)

ENDO. But this sitting here—surely you get hungry, don't you, day after day? Doesn't it make you hungry? Don't you ever feel you could sit down and enjoy a really good, well-cooked meal?

VISIONARY. I make a practice of eating far more than I need. And for that reason food is of no interest to me.

I eat merely to put food out of my mind. I eat all the time so that I shall not be preoccupied with supplying my bodily needs so far as food is concerned. It leaves my mind free.

ENDO. I see. And what form does this food generally take? Sandwiches? Fruit, perhaps?

VISIONARY. Not fruit.

ENDO. Sandwiches?

VISIONARY. Not sandwiches.

ENDO. Some other kind of food possibly . . . ?

VISIONARY. I hardly bother with food at all. I eat simply in order to put food out of my mind. We should see something happening very shortly. I don't think it's going to be very long now. We shall see them getting ready to pull the cord which will bring the veil fluttering down—and when that happens it's dark glasses for all of us. (*He picks up his newspaper and prepares to read*)

ENDO. The radiance.

VISIONARY. The what?

ENDO. Blinding everybody. The radiance of the light through the coloured glass you were speaking about, shining right into their eyes. Isn't that what you meant? Dark glasses to protect their eyes from the glare?

VISIONARY. The glare of what?

ENDO. When the curtain gets pulled down, or whatever it is, and the light starts streaming in. Through the new window—I thought you said a window was being unveiled in the south transept?

VISIONARY. Very shortly. It won't be long now. (*He transfers his attention to the newspaper*)

(ENDO *gives him up and stands looking down, too.*

    CEREBRO *enters down* R, *looking at the Visionary. He takes up a position* R *of Endo, leans on the pole and looks down into the hole*)

CEREBRO (*nodding towards the Visionary but looking at Endo*) We ought to be able to work something out if we put our minds to it. He must be waiting for *something*.

ENDO. He says he's queueing for dark glasses.

(CEREBRO *looks questioningly at Endo*)

For the radiance. In case he gets blinded.

CEREBRO (*looking across at the Visionary and then down into the hole*) Perhaps your eyesight's better than mine. Can *you* make out any radiance?

ENDO. They haven't unveiled the window, yet. Or so he says.

CEREBRO (*in mock comprehension*) Ah. (*He glances quickly at the Visionary, then dismisses him and looks intently down into the hole*)

(ENDO *looks intently down into the hole*)

There may be others in the shadows down there—but you can distinctly make out two people.

ENDO. They're playing some game.

(*There is a pause*)

CEREBRO. They're playing dominoes down there.

(*There is a pause*)

ENDO. In boxing gloves?

CEREBRO. They're playing dominoes. You can see the double six. There. In his left hand.

(*There is a pause*)

ENDO (*pointing*) Over there. Look. Coming out of the corner.

(*There is a pause*)

CEREBRO. He looks rather keyed up.

ENDO. I wonder if that could be the Battling Bombardier? Because if that's the Battling Bombardier, the other one must be Spider. (*He pauses*) Wait till he comes into the light. Yes. It is. It's Spider and the Battling Bombardier.

CEREBRO. Splendid! That's the boxing gloves accounted for.

(*There is a pause*)

ENDO. But not the shuttlecock.
CEREBRO. We'll come to that.

(*There is a pause*)

ENDO. You can always recognize the Battler . . .
CEREBRO. Snap!
ENDO. Snap! You could always recognize the Battling Bombardier even if you'd never seen him before because he's the only boxer who carries his own dartboard around with him.
CEREBRO. If the other one's Spider, he's just coming out of his corner.

(CEREBRO *and* ENDO *look down with intensified interest*)

ENDO. They'll probably limber up now with a brisk five minutes of Happy Families.

(SOMA *enters down* L *and stands* L *of the hole*)

SOMA. Keep your eye on Spider. He's the one to watch down there.

(*There is a pause*)

CEREBRO. Is he the one with the domino poised?
SOMA. That's only a blind. The domino's a blind. (*He pauses*) Any minute now he's going right in. (*He pauses*) The domino doesn't mean a thing. He's just waving that about for a blind. It's the seven of clubs— that's what you've got to keep your eye on.

(*There is a pause*)

CEREBRO. He seems to be threatening him with it, or something.
SOMA. I tell you it's a blind. It doesn't mean a thing. I've seen him do that for sometimes five minutes at a stretch. He'll come out brandishing a double six and he'll go on until he's got the other fellow practically mesmerized—in fact he is mesmerized more often than not the way Spider does it—and then whoosh! He's on him with Mr Rake the Gardener. It never fails.
ENDO. Snap!

CEREBRO. He seems to be biding his time at the moment.

SOMA. Snap! (*To Cerebro*) He knows what he's doing. (*He transfers his attention to Endo, as to a kindred spirit*) What do you think of him?

ENDO. He certainly seems to know what he's doing.

SOMA. Spider knows what he's doing, believe me. Once he's got his eye in I've known him trump every bishop from love-all to double twenty and not a pawn out of breath. He'd clear five foot six inches with as clean a backhand drive as you'd be likely to see in a lifetime of snooker. I've known people who claim to have seen him hold his opponent off with the ace of diamonds just long enough to re-load his dice, and then perhaps he'd huff him two or three times just for the hell of it, and then you'd see it. Then you'd see the real *coup de grace*— packed, sealed, addressed, delivered. First of all he'd come out behind his two rooks. He always did that— he always covered himself with his rooks—and he'd come out very slowly, very unconcerned as if it didn't matter today or tomorrow and then—you wouldn't see what happened next except that suddenly the other fellow wasn't there. Then you'd look again and he'd be picking himself up out of baulk with Mrs Grain the Grocer's Wife.

(SOMA *draws back and watches while both* ENDO *and* CEREBRO *become absorbed in what they can see in the hole. He looks suspiciously and with dislike towards the Visionary from time to time also*)

EEREBRO. Lead with your left!

(ENDO *looks sharply at Cerebro, then down, then back to Cerebro*)

CNDO. Lead with his what? He's in check.

(MRS ECTO *enters* L *and goes up the steps* L *on to the raised pavement. She carries a basket.*

MRS MESO *enters by the ramp up* R *on to the raised pavement. She carries a basket. The two women meet and cross each other on the raised pavement*)

Mrs Meso. Hallo, dear. I'm just off to get something for Ben's hands.

Mrs Ecto. How is he?

Mrs Meso. His hands are breaking out again.

Mrs Ecto. If only you could get him to wear bandages.

Mrs Meso. He will. He will wear bandages. There's no trouble at all getting Ben to wear bandages once his hands are healed up.

Mrs Ecto. Then it's too late.

Mrs Meso. You know how Ben goes on. He's not putting a lot of ointment and bandages on his hands when they're sore, as if he'd got no more individuality than the masses. No. Afterwards. Let them get nicely healed up and then he'll think about bandages.

Mrs Ecto. Ben's dead set on being different, isn't he?

Mrs Meso. He calls it showing initiative.

Mrs Ecto. Not like Sid.

Mrs Meso. He'll do anything rather than follow the herd.

Mrs Ecto. Sid just had another bad night worrying again about being so different from the people he sees round him.

Mrs Meso. Has he tried resembling anybody?

Mrs Ecto. He's tried all ways.

Soma. Snap!

Endo
Cerebro } (*almost simultaneously*) Snap!

Mrs Meso. They get very worked up, don't they?

Mrs Ecto. I wish I could get Sid interested.

Mrs Meso. Ben's too interested.

Mrs Ecto. He gets confused with the different rules. He can't seem to remember them like other people.

Mrs Meso. Ben can remember them, but he's got these ideas of his—or he pretends he has—and instead of keeping them to himself——

Endo. Look where he's left his ace—right over the pocket.

Mrs Meso. —instead of keeping his deviationist ideas

to himself he brings them out in front of people just to show how different he can be.

MRS ECTO. Like with Sid—it gives people a wrong impression.

ENDO. He's pausing to give his pawns a breather.

MRS MESO. It doesn't make him very popular at the works sometimes.

MRS ECTO. Sid hates it, of course. He's afraid people will think he's trying to be different deliberately.

ENDO. Beautiful! Did you see that?

MRS MESO. Ben's just the opposite.

ENDO. Did you see how he huffed his way out of that half-nelson? Beautiful!

MRS MESO. Nothing pleases Ben more than to have them calling him a deviationist.

CEREBRO. Don't you mean *bluffed* his way out of it?

ENDO. Spider could bluff his way out of anything.

MRS ECTO. That would upset Sid.

MRS MESO. He just likes watching people's faces when he shouts out his slogans.

ENDO. Heave!

MRS ECTO. I shouldn't have thought Ben was the type to be a deviationist.

MRS MESO. He isn't.

CEREBRO. They seem to be holding back.

ENDO. They are. All together now—heave! They're pulling their punches down there. And again—heave!

MRS MESO. Ben's no more interested in outdoor games than this railing. He's just as loyal at heart as anybody else to indoor games—but he can't resist making himself out to be different.

MRS ECTO. Sid's afraid of offending people. It doesn't matter with some things but people are funny about what they believe and what they don't believe.

ENDO. He needs more chalk on his Queen.

CEREBRO. Don't we all?

MRS MESO. I get cross with him sometimes.

MRS ECTO. Especially when it comes to indoor games.

MRS MESO. He sees them all looking down there and he's got no more sense than shout out things like—

(*sotto voce*) "Offside!" And "No ball!" And then he wonders why people take offence.

(ENDO *and* CEREBRO *move their heads left and right as if following a tennis ball*)

MRS ECTO. We're all entitled to have our own beliefs.

MRS MESO. I tell him sometimes, "It's in bad taste", but it makes no difference.

MRS ECTO. Sid flouts other people's beliefs, too—but it's always accidental. He never does it for the purpose. And he hates himself afterwards.

MRS MESO. Ben seems to glory in it.

(SOMA *begins calling the score*)

SOMA. Thirteen fourteen.

MRS ECTO. It's funny, isn't it—there's . . .

MRS MESO (*pointing towards the group round the hole*) The score.

MRS ECTO. Oh.

(MRS ECTO *and* MRS MESO *both stand as though for the National Anthem. Everyone joins in calling the score*)

ALL. Thirteen fifteen. Fourteen fifteen. Fifteen all.

(*There is a pause*)

Fifteen sixteen. Fifteen seventeen. Sixteen seventeen. Seventeen all.

(*There is a pause*)

Seventeen eighteen. Eighteen seventeen.

(*There is a pause*)

Eighteen all.

(*There is a pause*)

Eighteen nineteen. Eighteen twenty. Nineteen twenty. Twenty all.

(*There is a pause*)

One love—love two—game.

(CEREBRO *and* ENDO *shake hands. The* VISIONARY *yawns.* SOMA *crosses to the Visionary and pokes him*)

MRS ECTO. It's funny, really—there's Ben trying for all he's worth to be different——

MRS MESO. —and Sid trying to be the same.

MRS ECTO. He'd give anything. There's nothing Sid wouldn't give to be identical with somebody.

MRS MESO. Look!

(MRS MESO *draws* MRS ECTO's *attention to Soma.* ENDO *and* CEREBRO *draw together and occasionally exchange a remark*)

SOMA (*to the Visionary*) Is that a private vision you're indulging there?

MRS MESO. He's asking him questions.

VISIONARY. I just can't imagine where they're going to seat everybody—they're seating them in the nave but they won't see much from the nave.

SOMA. I thought my guess wasn't far out. (*He moves above the right end of the hole*)

MRS ECTO. He's telling him to move on.

VISIONARY. Except possibly some reflected light from one of the arches.

SOMA. It's strange how you can always tell a private vision.

VISIONARY. They'll see nothing at all of the window itself.

SOMA. You can tell it by the smell.

VISIONARY. Perhaps they intend some of them to stay behind so that they can look at it afterwards.

SOMA. It doesn't often fail in my experience.

VISIONARY. When the congregation has thinned out.

SOMA. If you were to have your hair cut and pressed your trousers once in a while, and then went and had a good bath, perhaps you'd get rid of some of your mucky ideas at the same time.

VISIONARY. It won't be long now.

SOMA. You might be able to see what's in front of your eyes like anybody else.

VISIONARY. I expect they want the sun full on the window. That's why we're having to wait.

SOMA. Instead of crawling off into a corner by yourself with a maggotty little private vision to keep you company.

VISIONARY. They'll no doubt time it very carefully.

SOMA (*moving down* R) What have you got against indoor games? Eh? Too wholesome?

(SOMA *exits down* R)

MRS ECTO. He's going off. They must be going to let him stay there.

MRS MESO. They probably know what they're doing. He'll be back if he gets up to anything.

(*The* VISIONARY *fumbles in his pockets*)

MRS ECTO (*nudging Mrs Meso; sotto voce*) Look. Feeling in his pocket.

(ENDO *and* CEREBRO *light cigarettes*)

MRS MESO. We'll see what he takes out.

(MRS ECTO *and* MRS MESO *move to the right end of the raised pavement. The* VISIONARY *takes out his pipe and lights it*)

MRS ECTO. What is it?
MRS MESO. He's lighting his pipe.
MRS ECTO. Oh.
ENDO. No. No, I shouldn't have thought golf.
CEREBRO (*straightening himself up*) Nevertheless that's what it is.
MRS MESO. Did I tell you Ben's been having trouble with his claustrophobia?
ENDO. In a hole that size?
MRS ECTO. Does Ben get it, too?
CEREBRO. Size is relative.
MRS MESO. He gets it with his ribs.
ENDO. I dare say.
MRS ECTO. It's being in the open brings it on with Sid.

ENDO. And a freshly dug hole at that.

MRS MESO. The first time he had it he went to the doctor with it.

ENDO (*moving to* L *of the hole*) You'd need golf links. You'd need fairways. You show me where the fairway is in a hole no bigger than a chest of drawers.

CEREBRO. A man is addressing a ball. And it seems a legitimate inference that a man with all the air of a golfer addressing a golf ball is in fact playing golf.

(ENDO *moves to Cerebro above the hole*)

Because once he swings the club he'll strike the ball and if we accept that a man swinging a golf club near a golf ball intends the consequences of his action, there can be no question but that the flight of the ball is part of a larger scheme of things which for convenience we call golf. If golf, then links; if links, then fairway.

(*There is a pause.* CEREBRO *crosses above Endo to* L *of him*)

ENDO. Unless he's just idly passing the time.

CEREBRO (*moving down* L) How long are the other golfers going to stand for that?

(CEREBRO *exits down* L. *There is a pause*)

ENDO (*moving down* L *and calling after Cerebro*) They'd have previous little choice, would they?

(ENDO *exits down* L)

MRS MESO (*resuming*) He went to Dr Bunch—he's been going to him for years—and complained about his ribs, and told him they seemed to be giving him claustrophobia. And do you know what he said to Ben? After all these years he's been going to him and all he could say was, "Surely you're not turning against your own ribs, Mr Meso?"

MRS ECTO. They don't know what it's like to have it.

MRS MESO. I was disgusted when Ben came home and told me.

MRS ECTO. Sid gets claustrophobia. He gets it coming

B

on whenever he's out in the open air for any length of time.

MRS MESO. That's because other people get it in confined spaces.

MRS ECTO. He never bothers with the doctor, now. When he feels it coming on he gets home as quickly as he can and says he's feeling a bit claustrophobic, and we've got a little broom cupboard—he just goes in there until it wears off.

MRS MESSO. I can always tell when Ben's got it coming on—he seems to want to have his ribs out of the way to give him some breathing space. He says it's like being behind bars. Although I think sometimes he puts it on a bit.

MRS ECTO. You can't blame him if he's trying to be unusual.

MRS MESO. It all helps to get him out of the rut, I suppose. And that's what he's set on. He's always on about us being in a cosmic rut.

MRS ECTO. I wish Sid was in a rut for his own sake.

MRS MESO. Hasn't he ever been in one?

MRS ECTO. He's been in several, but he's no sooner in than he's out again.

MRS MESO. He and Ben ought to change places.

MRS ECTO. People think he's going out of his way to be different—like with his claustrophobia—but what they don't realize is that he'd give anything to be similar.

MRS MESO. Is he making any headway at all?

MRS ECTO. He thinks there's a slight resemblance between him and a man he sees on the train sometimes, but he gets very disheartened.

MRS MESO. So does Ben.

MRS ECTO. I think at times he'd like to call the whole thing off.

MRS MESO. It doesn't get any easier as you get older.

(CEREBRO *enters down* L.
ENDO *follows him on*)

MRS ECTO. He'll be forty-five in the summer.

MRS MESO. Ben was forty-one in March.

Mrs Ecto. The fourth of August. He'll have his birthday over the bank holiday.

Mrs Meso. Ben's is on the twenty-second.

Voice (*off*) Fore!

(Cerebro *looks pointedly at* Endo, *who looks up and catches his eye*)

Endo. I'm not impressed by evidence from that quarter.

Mrs Meso. I must get along to the chemist's for Ben's lotion. If I can get him to use it.

Mrs Ecto. I'll come with you. I've got to collect the tickets for the outing from Mrs Backlog.

(Mrs Meso *and* Mrs Ecto *come down the steps* L, *cross above the hole and exit* R)

Endo. How do we know it isn't ventriloquial?

Cerebro (*looking down into the hole*) Your mind isn't very flexible, is it?

Endo. It's as flexible as it needs to be.

Cerebro. Is it? What's that, then?

Endo. It's a splendid stance. But it isn't a golfer's stance.

Cerebro. And that. See them? And there are some more.

Endo. There's no fairway; there's no clubhouse; there isn't even a single hole there, let alone eighteen— and you want me to see caddies and golfers all over the place. You'll never convince me. (*He moves* R)

Cerebro. And over there. What's that little group? They look remarkably like some sort of warm water fish.

(*There is a pause*)

Endo (*moving to the hole*) Warm water what?

Cerebro. Can't you see them, swimming about?

(*There is a pause.* Endo *looks alternately down and, bewildered, at Cerebro*)

A chub. A chub? That's not a warm water fish, surely? What's a chub doing here? Two chub. (*He pauses*) I wish I could make out what that is lying on the bottom.

(*There is a pause*)

ENDO. Aren't we going to have trouble reconciling this with golf?

CEREBRO. We don't have to. Do you know—I think it's a plaice.

(SOMA *enters down* R, *stands apart watching shrewdly for a few moments, then crosses to* L)

It is, too. This is going to need some thinking out.

ENDO. You mean we were wrong about the golf.

CEREBRO. About the what?

ENDO. I can't see how golf fits into all this.

CEREBRO. It was simply a working hypothesis. But it no longer fits the facts. You can discard golf.

(*There is a pause*)

ENDO. How on earth are we to know we're right about fish if we were wrong about golf?

CEREBRO. Golf's exploded as a theory now. Forget it.

(*There is a pause*)

ENDO (*pointing*) Guppies.

CEREBRO. I know—and look at that Golden Leopard. Some of these are tropical freshwater fish.

ENDO. Herrings? And mackerel? I thought they were saltwater fish.

CEREBRO. It's odd. And I've seen at least three trout —there's one there now, behind the gudgeon.

ENDO. They've no business in a tank with tropical fish. Look at the Black Widows. And the Bloodfins. They want seventy-five degrees Fahrenheit—that's what they're used to. They like it hot.

(*There is a pause*)

CEREBRO. We may have missed one or two, but I have just counted the species in there, and I make it fifteen; fifteen different species in one tank.

ENDO. What's the answer? (*He stands upright*)

CEREBRO. Our most immediate need is for a comprehensive hypothesis which will account for the presence in a single tank of fifteen mutually incompatible species of fish.

(*There is a pause*)

ENDO. Is it? (*He looks into the hole*)

(MRS MESO *and* MRS ECTO *enter* R *and cross to* L. MRS MESO *carries a large bottle of medicine.* MRS ECTO *carries a packet of tissues*)

MRS MESO (*as they cross*) He has to write everything down in case he forgets.

(CEREBRO *takes a notebook and pencil from his pocket, and writes, leaning against the steps*)

MRS ECTO. Sid's as bad. He can't remember a thing unless he makes a note about it first.

MRS MESO. If I hadn't kept Ben supplied with paper and pencil all these years, I don't know when Joan and Peter would have been born.

(MRS MESO *and* MRS ECTO *exit down* L)

CEREBRO (*moving to* L *of the hole*) Three tanks would be sufficient. I've got it down to three. A cold freshwater tank: that disposes of the river fish, except the tropical ones. For them we should need a tropical freshwater tank. And then a cold saltwater tank for the herrings and mackerel and so on. (*He pauses*) Three tanks. One tank superimposed on another. That's our answer. A freshwater tank. A saltwater tank. A tropical tank.

SOMA. A freshwater tank. A saltwater tank. A tropical aquarium.

ENDO. Side by side.

CEREBRO. One above another.

SOMA. Welded together.

ENDO. It plays ducks and drakes with the fish.

CEREBRO. Not one fish but is at its wits' end. Not one fish but would welcome some way out of a situation that

grows more impossible every moment. (*He puts the notebook and pencil in his pocket*) Move To hole.

SOMA. A freshwater tank, a saltwater tank, a tropical
aquarium.

ENDO. Side by side.

CEREBRO. One above another.

SOMA. Welded together.

ENDO. The tropical to the saltwater and the saltwater
to the freshwater and the freshwater to the tropical.

CEREBRO. The freshwater to the saltwater and the
saltwater to the tropical and the tropical to the freshwater.

(*There is a pause*)

I can't say for certain which one—but there's no doubt
in my mind that one of these tanks has been drinking.
(*He crosses above Endo to* R *of him*)

(MRS ECTO *and* MRS MESO *enter down* L *and pause at
the foot of the steps* L, *in conversation.* MRS ECTO *has a
loaf of bread.* MRS MESO *has a packet of cornflakes*)

MRS MESO. I can't imagine how Mrs Blacklog came
to think of a play like that for a Tuesday outing.

CEREBRO. Heavily.

MRS ECTO. It's a morbid play at the best of times, and
very nearly as morbid as the one we saw with Mrs
Lamprey, I expect.

MRS MESO. Wasn't that the one where they killed an
old man in his bed? A young couple?

ENDO. One can smell its breath.

CEREBRO. The other two are holding it up.

MRS ECTO. He was in the army. He kept seeing
daggers in the air.

ENDO. All three are drunk.

(SOMA *and* ENDO *lean back*)

MRS MESO. She was the one who really put him up to
it. And then trying to wash the blood off in her sleep.

CEREBRO. One is drunker than the other two. (*He
leans back*)

MRS ECTO. I thought she was a very unpleasant piece of work. I didn't take to her at all. She struck me as being two-faced all the way through. And the way she carried on when they found the old chap's body upstairs—as if she knew nothing about it.

ENDO. All three are equally drunk.

MRS MESO. Very two-faced.

CEREBRO. Two are drunker than the third.

MRS ECTO. It was her goading him into it that made him do it.

ENDO. One is as drunk as another.

MRS MESO. They all thought very highly of him to begin with, even the old chap. And then he met the gypsies, and what with his wife on at him all the time . . .

(SOMA *crosses to* C)

CEREBRO. Two are equally drunk while the other is stone-cold sober.

ENDO. Or almost equally drunk while the other is drunker than either.

MRS ECTO. And then of course once you've started you can't stop yourself. You've got to go on.

MRS MESO. It was a pity he ever met those gypsies.

CEREBRO. Or less drunk than both.

MRS ECTO. They must have known something. Unless they were in it in some way.

ENDO. Or as drunk as one but less drunk than the other.

MRS ECTO. I kept thinking one of them was going to trip over his sword or something.

MRS MESO. They get proper tuition for it.

CEREBRO. Or more drunk than one but not as drunk as the other.

MRS ECTO. It must be very awkward for them.

CEREBRO. Or conversely.

MRS ECTO. In those long robes, when they're in these old-fashioned plays.

SOMA. There are not three tanks but one. (*He moves in towards the hole*)

ENDO. Not one but three.

CEREBRO. Three in one and one in three.

MRS MESO. I suppose old Mrs Gridley won't be coming this time?

MRS ECTO. She can't get about much now.

SOMA. I believe——

ENDO
SOMA } (*together*) —in one aquarium——
CEREBRO

MRS MESO (*nudging Mrs Ecto*) "I believe . . ."

(*The* MEN *stand upright. The* WOMEN *put their baskets on the ground. All face the hole. The* VISIONARY *takes no notice*)

MRS ECTO. Oh.

ENDO

SOMA

CEREBRO

(*together; without a break*) —which was and is and shall be; in which shall be comprehended the sprat and the Black Widow; in it the sole and the carp shall swim together, the swordtail and water-flea; with the gudgeon shall float the mackerel, with the roach the guppy; duckweed shall be there, and foaming moss; neither shall the water at seventy-five degrees Fahrenheit be at variance with the water at forty degrees Fahrenheit, or eschew it. And the freshwater shall be salt and the saltwater fresh, and no distinction shall be made between them, for all are of one aquarium and there is no other aquarium, but this.

(*The* WOMEN *pick up their baskets*)

MRS ECTO. It would be just as well if she didn't come if it's going to be another play about people murdering each other for what they can get out of it.

CEREBRO (*nodding towards the Visionary*) He looks very absorbed in something.

ENDO. He thinks he's watching the dance of the seven veils or something down there.

MRS MESO. They're talking about that tramp again.

CEREBRO. Imagination, but no intellectual discipline.
ENDO. He hasn't had a bath since he took up his pitch over there.

(ENDO *and* CEREBRO *move up* R)

CEREBRO. He's harmless.
SOMA. He's dangerous. (*He moves* L)
ENDO ⎱ (*together; as though by a reflex*) He's danger-
CEREBRO ⎰ ous.

(ENDO *and* CEREBRO *exit up* R. MRS MESO *and* MRS ECTO *move above the hole*)

MRS MESO. Are we going to be left alone with *him*?
MRS ECTO (*to Soma*) Do you really think he's got a *private* vision?
SOMA. Can't you see it in the way he's sitting there? He's got private vision written all over him.
MRS ECTO. I can't think why he's not stopped.
SOMA. We're watching him. It might be better if you ladies didn't give him any encouragement—not that you'd be at all likely to do that, I expect.
MRS MESO. Certainly not!
SOMA. If he gives you any trouble, I shan't be far away.

(SOMA *exits down* L. MRS MESO *and* MRS ECTO *move down* L *of the hole*)

MRS MESO. Flouting everybody's beliefs.
MRS ECTO. If he doesn't believe in the aquarium, what *does* he believe in?

(*There is a pause*)

MRS MESO. Have you ever thought of trying to get Sid breathing properly?
MRS ECTO. I've tried everything, Gladys. It isn't for want of trying that Sid isn't normal, believe me.
MRS MESO. I thought perhaps if he could get his breathing straight it might be a start for him.
MRS ECTO. He's out of step with it—he's breathing in

all the time when he should be breathing out and that puts him out all the way along. He can't get back into phase with it except by breathing in twice running.

Mrs Meso. Or breathing out. He could surely breathe *out* twice running?

Mrs Ecto. I've tried him with that, too. Once he starts breathing out he has to go on till he's finished. And then when he tries to breathe out a second time——

Mrs Meso. —he's got no more air left.

(Cerebro *enters down* R, *moves above the hole and stands looking down into it.*
        Endo *follows Cerebro on and stands* R *of him looking down into the hole*)

Mrs Ecto. Not a scrap. And then of course he gets disillusioned.

Mrs Meso. I wonder what it is they find so interesting down there.

(Mrs Meso *draws* Mrs Ecto *to* L *of the hole where they both remain looking down into it.*
        Soma *enters down* L *and stands above the hole,* L *of Cerebro*)

(*To Mrs Ecto*) He's tapping on the pipes.

Mrs Ecto. Perhaps he wants to get out.

Mrs Meso. It's the way they have of signalling to each other. He's tapping out a message to someone in the next cell.

(*There is a pause*)

Cerebro. He's signalling.

(*There is a pause*)

Endo. He's tapping on the pipes.

(*There is a pause*)

Cerebro. He's signalling.
Endo. He's tapping on the pipes.
Soma. He's sending a message.

Endo. There's someone in the next cell and he's sending a message.

(*There is a pause*)

Soma. He's in solitary confinement.
Cerebro. He wants to make contact.
Endo. He's tapping out a message.

(*There is a pause*)

Cerebro. He's in a cell six foot by nine.
Soma. He's pacing backwards and forwards.
Endo. He's tapping on the pipes.
Cerebro. He wants the exercise.
Soma. He's here for six months.
Cerebro. He's been given nine years.
Endo. He's tapping out a message.
Soma. He's on Number One diet.
Endo. He's signalling on the pipes.
Cerebro. He's using a fork.
Endo. He's tapping with a spoon.
Cerebro. He's on Number Three diet.
Soma. He's pacing up and down.
Endo. He's been given solitary confinement.
Soma. He's got seven years.
Endo. He's in for three months.
Soma. He's trying to make contact.
Cerebro. He's in a cell eight foot by twelve.
Soma. He's being punished.
Endo. He's tapping on the pipes.
Soma. He's pacing.
Endo. He's tapping. They found him breaking and entering and now they've put him inside.
Soma. He has done wrong, and he has chosen to do it illegally.
Cerebro. It is the duty of every one of us to avoid those crimes we know to have been blacklisted.
Soma. To act otherwise is evil. More than that, it is a breach of the law. (*He crosses to* L)
Endo. How, when evil takes such form as this, can we give our approval to it?

SOMA. No man must be allowed to do wrong who cannot do it acceptably. (*He crosses down* R *of the hole and looks into it*)

(*There is a pause*)

MRS MESO. He's pacing.

MRS ECTO. He's tapping on the pipes.

MRS MESO. He should be made to empty his slops. (*She sits on the oil bin down* L *of the hole*)

CEREBRO (*moving down* L) I hold no brief for sadism, but I can't help thinking a good dose of old-fashioned torture would have a lot to be said for it.

MRS MESO. They should be making him empty his slops.

ENDO. I personally am a firm believer in live and let live and always have been, but all the same there are a good few people who'd be better out of the way in my opinion.

MRS ECTO. Let him empty his slops.

SOMA. The last thing I want is to sound vindictive, but just about the most salutary thing that could happen to us would be a return to the days when you could occasionally see people hanged, drawn and quartered.

ENDO (*moving down* R) I'm always a bit suspicious personally of any argument that's too much on the watertight side as to the facts and figures when punishment is at stake.

CEREBRO. I've got no more time for retribution than the next fellow, or anything remotely suggestive of it as far as that goes; God forbid that we should get back to an eye for an eye and a tooth for a tooth or any of that nonsense in this day and age—but all the same you can't get away from it that with things as they are it's a damned sound principle to act on and I for one am all for it.

ENDO. To the stake!

MRS MESO. Let him empty his slops first.

MRS ECTO. Let him empty his slops.

ENDO. All my life I've been passionately on the side of those who have fought in season and out of season against the barbarity of capital punishment; nevertheless it does seem to me that by doing away with it we're going dangerously far in the opposite direction.

SOMA. A little intelligent bloodthirstiness is all that's wanted.

CEREBRO. To the hulks. (*He moves and stands below the hole*)

ENDO. Transportation! (*He moves and stands* R *of Cerebro below the hole*)

(*There is a pause*)

MRS ECTO. Bring back the rack!

(*There is a pause*)

SOMA. Break him on the wheel!

ENDO. To the hulks!

MRS MESO (*rising*) Let him empty his slops and break him on the wheel!

MRS ECTO. Burn him! Burn him at the stake! (*She moves and stands above the hole*)

(*There is a pause*)

ENDO. Bring back the rack!

(*There is a pause*)

SOMA. The rope! (*He crosses above the hole and stands up* L *of it*)

ENDO. The lash!

SOMA. The cat!

CEREBRO. The club!

(*There is a pause*)

MRS ECTO. Bring back the harpoon!

(*There is a pause*)

SOMA. Bring back the cudgel!

CEREBRO. The poleaxe!

ENDO. The battering ram!

SOMA. The gallows!

ENDO. The gibbet!

CEREBRO. The Gatling gun!

(*There is a pause*)

MRS ECTO. Let him empty his slops and then bring back the shillelagh!

CEREBRO. Stand clear!

(*They all scatter*)

SOMA. (*warningly*) Slops! (*He moves and stands up* R *of the hole, looking at it*)

ENDO. Retribution!

(*There is a flash, followed by a loud explosion. The* VISIONARY *sips a cup of tea*)

SOMA (*after a pause*) There, but for the grace of God, went my slops.

ENDO. He has paid the penalty. (*He pauses*) He's emptied his slops, now.

MRS ECTO. Right to the last slop he maintained his innocence.

ENDO. They're emptied now. There's nothing more to be done or said now.

(*There is a pause*)

MRS MESO. A pity he and a few more like him weren't made to empty more slops when they were youngsters.

MRS ECTO. Poor devil. He made a very fine splash at the end.

(*There is a pause*)

ENDO. He's paid the price. He's emptied his slops. It's time we were going.

(*All except* CEREBRO *begin to disperse, moving off in different directions and speaking in more subdued tones*)

CEREBRO. Nothing in his slops became him like th emptying them.

SOMA. Justice.

MRS MESO. There will be other battles against evil.

SOMA. Other battles, other slops.

ENDO. Transportation.

SOMA. Retribution.
ENDO. To the hulks.

(ENDO *exits down* R. MRS MESO *and* MRS ECTO *stand down* L *of the hole*)

MRS ECTO. To the hulks.
SOMA. Justice.

(SOMA *exits down* R)

CEREBRO (*absent-mindedly*) Well done the state. (*He moves, stands above the right end of the hole and looks with intent curiosity at the Visionary, trying to discover what it is he can see*)

(MRS MESO *points out the encounter to* MRS ECTO *and they both stand watching*)

(*To the Visionary*) They tell me you're watching the dance of the seven veils. But I don't suppose that comes within a mile of the truth. Does it?
VISIONARY. All one needs is patience. There has to be delay. It's inevitable. But everything is ready. The cord has been rigged up—it only has to be pulled when the time is ripe. We shall see something soon.
CEREBRO. No-one else is going to see it. And you yourself don't see it, either, except in your imagination. It bears no relationship to reality.
VISIONARY. Wait till the sun strikes the glass.

(CEREBRO *gives him up, lights a cigarette, then sits on the steps* L *and writes in his notebook*)

MRS MESO. Ben's got a new idea he's going to try out Christmas. He's got it all worked out. He's going to start us all off next year on a different kind of calendar.
MRS ECTO. I wish Sid could make up his mind what to do about a calendar. (*She moves below the hole*)
MRS MESO (*following Mrs Ecto*) He thinks it's time we all launched out a bit, instead of fifty-two weeks, fifty-two weeks, fifty-two weeks every blessed year as if we were all slaves of the calendar.

(Mrs Ecto *lights a cigarette for herself*)

Mrs Ecto. I never know with Sid whether it's summer or winter—he seems to chop and change with his calendar from one day to another.

Mrs Meso. Yes. Ben isn't going to change about in the middle of the year, though. He says he's going to cut his year down to fifty-one weeks and show a bit of independence.

Mrs Ecto. He's certainly got initiative.

Mrs Meso (*crossing to* r) Ben's got initiative.

(Mrs Ecto *follows Mrs Meso to* r)

He's got initiative for ten if only he'd use it properly.

(Mrs Meso and Mrs Ecto *exit down* r.

Endo *enters* r, *holding between finger and thumb of his left hand, a pickled onion. With his right hand he pats one pocket after another as though for matches with which to light a cigarette. He sees Cerebro and crosses above the hole to him*)

Endo. I wonder if you could oblige me with a fork?

(Cerebro *hardly looks up, takes a small fork from his breast pocket and hands it to Endo*)

Cerebro. Of course.

Endo. Thanks. Have an onion?

Cerebro. I don't eat, thanks.

Endo. Sensible fellow. (*He spears the onion with the fork, puts the onion in his mouth then throws the fork, like a spent match, into the hole*) Thanks for the fork. (*He turns to go*)

Cerebro (*jumping to his feet*) That's a dangerous thing to do. (*He goes to the hole and looks down*) You could easily do some damage with that.

Endo (*stopping and turning*) Damage? A fork?

Cerebro (*looking at Endo; severely*) It's a fork, now, but what happens when the fork becomes a knife?

Endo (*with a sceptical laugh*) That sort of thing couldn't happen here, old man.

Cerebro (*looking into the hole*) No? Come over here, then.

(ENDO *approaches with a kind of jaunty scepticism and looks at the hole. His expression changes suddenly to one of dumbfounded horror. He looks up almost appealingly at Cerebro, then down again. There is a pause.*

SOMA *enters unnoticed down* L *and joins Cerebro and Endo. He carries an umbrella*)

ENDO. It's a bloodstained knife!

(SOMA *hangs his umbrella on the pole*)

CEREBRO. It's ritual murder!
SOMA. It's human sacrifice!

(*There is a pause*)

ENDO. It's a great responsibility. They'll have it on their conscience.
CEREBRO. One at a time.
ENDO. Altogether.
CEREBRO. Individually.
ENDO. As a body.
CEREBRO. Singly.
ENDO. Corporately.
CEREBRO. My turn tonight, yours tomorrow.

(MRS MESO *and* MRS ECTO *enter down* R)

MRS MESO. So we've all got to try it out next year.
MRS ECTO. You'll be able to see how it goes.
MRS MESO. He's got seven different calendars worked out, so we should be able to find one to suit us from all those.
CEREBRO. They'll shoulder the burden.
ENDO. They'll share the load.
MRS MESO. He's just waiting now. He's waiting for Christmas Eve. He's going to ring in the New Year at midnight on Christmas Eve, and then he'll stand back and see what happens.
MRS ECTO. It might work out very nicely for you.
MRS MESO. I told him it means we're going to find ourselves a week earlier than everyone else all next year.

C

MRS ECTO. Sid's never in the same week for more than two minutes together.

MRS MESO. They ought to change places.

ENDO. They're priests.

SOMA. They're naked.

ENDO. They're priests with knives.

MRS ECTO. Isn't it going to throw him out with his seasons?

MRS MESO. Eventually it will. But seasons don't worry him much.

CEREBRO. It's ritual murder.

ENDO. It's human sacrifice.

CEREBRO. It's horrible.

MRS MESO. What he really wants eventually if he can keep at it is to gradually force New Year's Eve back to January the first.

MRS ECTO. Single-handed?

MRS MESO. He won't pay an assistant.

ENDO. We've no time to lose.

CEREBRO. We stayed too long talking.

ENDO. We're late on the scene.

CEREBRO. We took the wrong turning.

ENDO. We shall have to step it out.

CEREBRO. We shall never make it.

MRS ECTO. I suppose it's the originality of it that appeals to Ben.

MRS MESO. Oh, yes—the money doesn't interest him.

SOMA. They're Asian.

ENDO. They're Eastern. (*He stands upright*)

SOMA. They're Asian hordes. (*He stands upright*)

(*There is a pause*)

CEREBRO. We're all Democrats together, but this is sinister. (*He stands upright*)

(*There is a pause*)

ENDO. We must get out the reference books.

CEREBRO (*to Soma*) We must look up hara-kiri.

ENDO. Send for *Whittaker's*.

SOMA. Look up voodoo.

Endo. Send for dictionaries.
Cerebro. They're atavistic.
Soma. Send for maps.
Cerebro. For dictionaries.
Endo. Encyclopaedias.
Cerebro. They're killing their victim.
Endo. They're in a trance.
Cerebro. It's a ritual trance.
Endo. It's fetishistic.
Cerebro. Look up Mau-Mau.
Soma. Send for textbooks.
Cerebro. Look up Mau-Mau under tribal customs.
Soma. It's Oriental.
Endo. It's superstitious.
Soma. It's far from legal.
Cerebro. There's been a White Paper.
Endo. A Royal Commission.
Soma. A Select Committee.

(*There is a pause*)

Endo. Sound the alarm.

(Mrs Meso *and* Mrs Ecto *cross to the steps and go up to the raised pavement. There is a pause*)

Cerebro (*crossing to* R) What are our leaders doing?
Endo. We must act.
Cerebro (*moving up* R) Where are our leaders?
Endo (*following Cerebro*) Action.
Cerebro (*moving to* R *of the hole*) Alert our leaders.
Endo (*moving to* L *of Cerebro*) There is no time to be lost.
Cerebro (*moving down* C) Our leaders must be briefed.
Endo (*following Cerebro*) It's pagan.
Cerebro (*circling down* R) It's reprehensible.
Soma (*moving* L *in a figure of eight*) The Press has come out against it.
Cerebro. It's a bestial ritual.
Endo. They're burning widows.
Soma (*moving down* LC) They're asking questions in the House.

CEREBRO (*crossing to* C) They're Ku Klux Klan.

ENDO (*moving to* R *of Cerebro*) They're burning widows.

CEREBRO (*crossing to* R) We're all Anglo-Saxons together but this is suttee.

ENDO (*following Cerebro*) We must get out the regulations.

CEREBRO (*circling up* R *to* R) They're burning their victims.

SOMA (*moving up* LC) We must get out the regulations.

ENDO. Shame on the fire brigade.

CEREBRO (*moving down* R) We must starve them of victims.

ENDO (*crossing down* L) Thus far and no farther.

CEREBRO (*crossing to* C) We must harass their supply lines.

SOMA (*moving up* C) Stop them at source.

(ENDO *backs to* C, *bumps into Cerebro and bounces off him*)

CEREBRO (*crossing above Endo to* LC) Blockade them.

SOMA (*moving above the hole*) An embargo on victims.

(*A kind of Crusading fervour has taken hold of all three men, who now begin marching in all directions shouting slogans and information.* SOMA *repeatedly takes single steps towards each of the four points of the compass in turn, shouting "Forward" at each step*)

ENDO (*marching* R) Death to the Asian hordes.

CEREBRO (*marching* L) Blood will have blood.

ENDO (*marching* C) Death to the Wogs.

CEREBRO (*marching* C *and facing Endo*) To the ramparts.

ENDO. To the barricades.

CEREBRO. To the ramparts.

ENDO ⎫ (*together; stamping and turning to face front*)
CEREBRO ⎭   Into battle!

CEREBRO. Any more for the ramparts?

ENDO. Bastions over there—barricades this way.

CEREBRO. On to victory. Barricades on the left—ramparts—ramparts straight ahead. (*He marches* L *to Soma and bounces him to* R)

ENDO (*marching* R) Onward.

CEREBRO (*marching* L) Straight ahead.
ENDO (*marching up* R) Am I right for the bastions?
CEREBRO (*backing to* C *above the hole*) Fork left.

(SOMA *directs Cerebro up* R)

ENDO (*marching* C *above the hole*) Bear right.
CEREBRO (*marching down* R) Hard to port.
ENDO. Port to starboard.
CEREBRO (*marching down* C) Taxi!
ENDO (*marching up* L) Helm-a-lee.
CEREBRO (*marching down* L) To the ramparts. Taxi!
ENDO (*marching down* L) Bastions this way, please.
CEREBRO. Into battle. Taxi! Taxi!

(CEREBRO *exits up* R)

ENDO. This way to the bastions. Mind your heads on
the cobblestones, please. Follow me.

(ENDO *exits down* L. *There is a pause*)

MRS ECTO (*nodding towards Soma*) Very single-minded.

(SOMA *crosses below the hole to* C.
ENDO *enters down* L *and meets Soma* C)

SOMA (*grasping Endo's hand*) Harry!
ENDO. It must be sixteen years and a month since we
met, counting leap years.
SOMA. I think it might be as well not to count the
leap years.
ENDO. Do you know, I remember your name as if it
was yesterday—but I'm damned if I haven't completely
forgotten your face for a moment.
SOMA. Let me show you a photograph. (*He takes a
photograph from his pocket and hands it to Endo*)
ENDO (*looking at the photograph and then at Soma*) Ah!
This explains everything. What happened to the beard?
SOMA. I had it shaved off two or three years ago. At
Somerset House.
ENDO. It's not often I forget a face. I knew there must
be some reason. (*He looks at the photograph*) I remember
when this was taken. It was on the river.

SOMA. Twickenham. Nineteen thirty-six.

ENDO. This was the day we had the accident with the roll of carpet. When Steve and Lottie broke it off.

SOMA. That's it. We were all soaked through—remember?

ENDO. July the ninth, nineteen thirty-six. I've got it in an old diary somewhere.

SOMA. I've written the date on the back.

ENDO (*looking at the back of the photograph*) "July the ninth, nineteen thirty-six." You must have written this at the time. (*He returns the photograph to Soma*)

SOMA. As soon as I got the prints.

ENDO. You didn't let any grass grow under your feet, did you? Well, now we've run into each other after all this time, what do you say to inspecting the drains?

SOMA. Splendid.

(ENDO *and* SOMA *exit briskly down* L. *The* VISIONARY *looks at his watch, then peers down the hole.*

A WORKMAN, *carrying a bag of tools and a coil of wire emerges from the hole. He talks in loud disgust as he clambers out.*

CEREBRO *enters down* R)

WORKMAN. Cables! Junction box! Electricity! (*He turns to go off* R *and encounters Cerebro*) You never had any of this ruddy caper back in the Ice Age.

(*The* WORKMAN *exits down* R. CEREBRO *approaches the hole and looks thoughtfully down.*

ENDO *and* SOMA *enter down* L. ENDO *is slightly tipsy*)

SOMA. And this looks like another drain.

ENDO. Then why aren't we inspecting it? (*He goes impetuously forward, looks perfunctorily down the hole then turns to Soma*) Dam' fine drain, sir!

CEREBRO (*with some distaste*) I'm afraid this is a junction box.

(ENDO *seems to be brought up short by this statement and turns uncertainly to* SOMA, *who, together with* MRS MESO *and* MRS ECTO, *seems equally shocked by it*)

ENDO. What was that word you used?

CEREBRO. Junction box. There's just a junction box down there and some cables for electricity.

(*There is a pause*)

SOMA. I'd like to challenge you on that, sir.

CEREBRO (*slightly taken aback*) Oh. Well, challenge away, then. But I should have thought that thing down there was what you'd have to challenge. If that isn't a junction box and some electric cables the way you're looking at it, then obviously there's no more to be said.

ENDO (*to Soma; by way of invoking his support*) He can cut out that word "junction box" for a start. It's a word I've never heard before and I'm not going to stand here and listen to it being used.

MRS MESO (*to Mrs Ecto*) They hold nothing sacred.

SOMA. It seems to me quite pitiful that anyone can really seriously maintain that beliefs which for centuries have sustained men through all kinds of tribulations, and have uplifted his spirit in good times and in bad, can be explained away like this—can be reduced to a junction box and a few cables. It's pitiful. Pitiful and at the same time dangerous. Because what happens if these ideas begin to take hold? What sort of anchor have you got left?

MRS ECTO. They just seem to want to tear down everything.

ENDO (*moving to Cerebro*) Some of you people wouldn't last five minutes if you had to stand up in a public debate against people who know what they're talking about.

(*There is a pause*)

SOMA. And this word "junction box". Does it mean anything? Or is it just a new name for something we've been looking at all along?

CEREBRO. It does have meaning—a very definite meaning. Though it doesn't make a great deal of difference to what's down there, whether you call it by that name or another one. We call it a junction box because that happens to be a useful and convenient term for it—

but any other name would do almost equally well. We
know quite a lot about it, too. We know what its function
is and we know what would be the immediate and the
long-term effects of removing it. We could fairly easily—
if you particularly asked us to do so—find out who put
the junction box here and when. We can tell at roughly
what date the modifications incorporated in this type
were adopted as standard, and we can tell you to what
extent they represent an improvement on the old type.
There is very little in fact that we don't know about the
junction box.

(*There is a pause*)

SOMA (*at large*) He wants to take away all the mystery,
all the poetry, all the enchantment. And what does he
put in its place? A junction box. That and a few cables.
    ENDO. What sort of a philosophy is that for a man to
live his life by?
    SOMA. It's bleak, it's repellent, and the sooner we
reaffirm the great truths of the past the better for all of
us.
    ENDO. The water!
    SOMA. The ritual!
    ENDO. The snooker!
    SOMA. The golf!

(*There is a pause*)

    ENDO. The shimmering!
    SOMA. The solitude!
    VISIONARY. The translucence!
    ENDO. The trumps!

(*There is a pause*)

(*Half to himself*) What was it they used to say about
truth? Truth at the bottom of a well.
    SOMA. This isn't a well—there's no well here. So
don't come out with any nonsense about truth lying at
the bottom of a well. This is just a hole in the ground.
Remember that. *Magna est veritas.*
    CEREBRO. And of course we know quite a bit about

the cables, too. There appear to be three, but we're not sure yet whether there's a fourth cable unaccounted for.

Mrs Ecto (*in a momentary access of elation*) Truth shall flourish out of the earth!

(*Mrs Ecto encounters Mrs Meso's glance and carries it off as best she can*)

Endo. And what does it turn out to be? What does the truth turn out to be? A junction box and some cables!

(*There is a pause*)

Soma (*his resistance crumbling; sulkily*) Which _are_ the cables?

Cerebro. You can see them running out from the junction box in the middle.

Soma. They're more than two inches across.

Cerebro. They'll be for telephones in all probability.

Mrs Meso (*to Mrs Ecto*) If they're two inches thick they're going to eat up the conversation.

Endo. I wonder how much better off we are than when we believed in fish and voodoo and snooker. (*He blows his nose*)

Cerebro. What would you say to a fourth cable?

Endo. I'd say it was nonsense.

Cerebro. Nevertheless a fourth cable is present.

(*Soma's attention is attracted to the Visionary. His interest during Cerebro's exposition will be in its effect on the Visionary, whom he watches intently*)

Soma (*glancing momentarily at Cerebro, and then sharply back to the Visionary*) Go ahead.

Cerebro. We have all seen three—or what appear to be three—cables and have assumed these to be going *into* the junction box. All three are in fact coming *out*. Since this is so, these cables are parting from one another and there cannot therefore be said to have been a join. But by definition a join must have taken place, since without a join there can be no junction box.

(*The* VISIONARY *yawns*)

A fourth cable is therefore to be inferred.

(SOMA *crosses above the Visionary to* R *of him*)

I submit that this in fact exists, and that it enters the junction box from the only side on which we are unable to see it enter—from underneath.

ENDO. A very impressive piece of reasoning. (*He crosses to Cerebro and shakes his hand*)

SOMA. Very impressive indeed. But not apparently to our friend over there.

ENDO. Most impressive.

SOMA (*to the Visionary*) Some of us have been watching you.

ENDO. Rather a brilliant imaginative leap, if I may say so. To that fourth cable.

SOMA. We've been watching you pretty closely for some time.

VISIONARY. It shouldn't be long now.

ENDO. Brilliant!

SOMA. I don't know what it is you're looking at, but there are others besides me who have the strongest possible objection to having to watch you watch it.

VISIONARY. I can't imagine how they're going to find room for any more people.

SOMA. I'm all for everybody having the right to his own opinions. Within limits he's entitled to believe what he likes as far as I'm concerned.

VISIONARY. Even the nave is filling up, and they'll be able to see precious little from the nave.

SOMA. I believe in a man being free to hold whatever opinion he likes as long as he doesn't abuse that freedom.

ENDO. Just look at that cable. Look at the direction it takes!

SOMA. Once he begins to abuse it by setting his face against the cables and the junction box for the sake of some unsavoury little opinion of his own—we know exactly the kind of man we're dealing with.

ENDO. Amazing!

(MRS MESO *and* MRS ECTO *cross to* L *of the hole*)

Just think of all the millions of directions that cable could have taken. And yet out of all those directions— and this is what I find so staggering—out of all those millions of directions, which one does it take? It takes that one.

MRS ECTO. I wouldn't like to think of Sid being stranded in the middle of all those directions.

MRS MESO. Ben would be in his element.

MRS ECTO. He wouldn't know which way to turn.

(SOMA *crosses to the foot of the steps* L)

MRS MESO. You can't tell. He might even make a better job of it than Ben, once he got down to it.

MRS ECTO. Not Sid. He'd run through the best part of a million directions before you could turn round.

MRS MESO. As long as they get the electricity.

(SOMA *pauses at the steps and looks at Endo*)

ENDO (*ruminating at large*) I suppose it's been there all the time, really. I suppose there's always been a junction box.

(SOMA *goes up the steps to* C *of the raised pavement and hangs his hat and umbrella on the railings*)

And cables. They were there in the aquarium; they were there in the billiards and the chess. Right from the very beginning there's been the everlasting electricity behind it all.

SOMA. The junction box is electricity made manifest.

(*The* VISIONARY *continues to remain oblivious of all except his vision. The others group themselves around Soma and prepare to listen.* MRS MESO *stands* L *of the hole.* MRS ECTO *sits on the oil bin.* CEREBRO *stands up* R *of the hole.* ENDO *stands up* L *of it. They all face Soma*)

We are accustomed on Generating Sunday to think especially of the principle of electro-magnetic induction.

Nevertheless the subject that I have chosen to speak first
to you about today is another one; for as we look down
on the countless strands twisting through endless cables
and ponder once again the mystery which we call Con-
fusion, it is fitting that we should remember those to
whom the mystery is not revealed, and especially those
who, though they see only darkness and the disposal of
sewage, will sometimes seem to talk knowledgeably of the
things of the cavity. You may hear talk of subsidence,
and of main drainage. You will hear people say: This
leads down to the cellar behind The Mortal Man. They
may use words which perhaps seemed strange to you
when you heard them for the first time, or read them in
your newspaper, but it is for this very reason that you
must be particularly on your guard. Because we are
made so that we sometimes in these matters mistakenly
turn away from what has become familiar, allowing ourselves to be deluded by the false because it is new. When
therefore we come together on certain days of the year
around the cavity, we do so in order to strengthen our
faith against those doubts by which it is assailed. For
each time we draw near to the cavity and together peer
down into the depths, we are not only giving expression
by that act to the unquenchable curiosity that is in us,
but we are at the same time reaffirming the truth of the
eternal and inscrutable paradox—that it is upon this cavity that we build our faith. And it is for this reason that
on Generating Sunday at the same time as we celebrate
the electro-magnetic induction of our own special scien-
tist and electrician, Michael Faraday, we also remember
the Excavation of the Rectangular Cavity. In the name
of Volta, Ampere and Galvani.

(SOMA *picks up his hat and umbrella and exits up* R.

ENDO *and* CEREBRO *exit thoughtfully* R. MRS MESO
moves L. MRS ECTO *rises, follows Mrs Meso but pauses
and looks back at the* VISIONARY *who settles down to sleep
again*)

VISIONARY (*in a self-absorbed undertone*) . . . whose quote
or rather misquote many-coloured glass will God willing

in all probability stain the white radiance of eternity unquote to the everlasting glory of God. God willing in a
short time now. In the south transept.

Mrs Meso (*to Mrs Ecto; as she goes*) He should be put
away.

Mrs Meso *exits down* L. Mrs Ecto *shakes her head
and exits slowly down* L *as—*

the Curtain *falls*

FURNITURE AND PROPERTY LIST

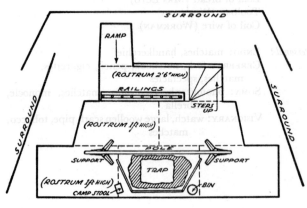

On stage: 2 wood tripods
Barrier pole
Tubular barriers
Oil drum
2 oil lamps
Red flag
Folding campstool
Blanket
Air cushion
Haversack. *In it:* books, writing-pad, pencil
Alarm clock
Newspaper
Vacuum-flask of tea

Off stage: Shopping basket (MRS MESO)
Shopping basket. *In it:* 2 tickets, packet of cigarettes,
    matches (MRS ECTO)
Large bottle of medicine (MRS MESO)
Packet of tissues (MRS ECTO)
Pickled onion (ENDO)
Packet of cornflakes (MRS MESO)
Loaf of bread (MRS ECTO)
Toolbag (WORKMAN)
Coil of wire (WORKMAN)

Personal: ENDO: matches, handkerchief
CEREBRO: fork, notebook, pencil, cigarettes,
    matches, spectacles
SOMA: photograph, cigarettes, matches, monocle,
    umbrella
VISIONARY: watch, large woollen scarf, pipe, tobacco,
    matches

EFFECTS PLOT